THE
SECRET
OF THE AGES

T0145757

THE
SECRET
OF THE AGES

by Robert Collier

The Legendary Success Formula

Abridged and Introduced
by Mitch Horowitz

T0145868

THE CONDENSED CLASSICS LIBRARY™

Published by Gildan Media LLC
aka G&D Media.
www.GandDmedia.com

The Secret of the Ages was originally published in 1925 as
The Book of Life.
It appeared under its current title in 1926, and was revised by
the author in 1948.
G&D Media Condensed Classics edition published 2018
Abridgement and Introduction copyright © 2015 by Mitch
Horowitz

FIRST EDITION: 2018

Cover design by David Rheinhardt of Pyrographx

Interior design by Meghan Day Healey of Story Horse, LLC.

ISBN: 978-1-7225-0054-2

Contents

What Is the "Secret of the Ages"?

Robert Collier was born to a prosperous Irish immigrant household in St. Louis, Missouri, in 1885. As the nephew of publishing magnate P.F. Collier, the boy was part of a socially prominent family—but his early life was marked by tragedy. Robert's parents often lived apart and his mother died when he was eleven. He spent much of the remainder of his youth in boarding schools.

As Collier neared adulthood, however, he discovered a world of possibilities. He trained for the priesthood and, deciding it wasn't for him, tried his hand as a mining engineer, journalist, advertising man, and publisher.

Collier's prospects dimmed in the early 1920s when he suffered a chronic and debilitating case of food poisoning. For months the illness sapped his energies and resisted treatment. Searching for a cure, Collier dedicated himself to the study of Christian Science, prayer healing, autosuggestion, and New Thought, a popular metaphysical movement based on principle that *thoughts are causative.* Robust mental imaging, went the New Thought gospel, could restore health.

Using his new psycho-spiritual methods, Collier recovered. He came to wonder: Could the same mind-power metaphysics work for other needs, such as money and career success? Collier threw himself into studying the higher dimensions of the mind. The writer came to believe that as God had created man in His own image, so could man, through his powers of mental imaging, function as a creator within his earthly sphere of existence.

In 1926 Collier mapped out his program in a pamphlet series called *The Secret of the Ages.* He had actually begun publishing his series the prior year when, perhaps thinking of his miracle recovery, he called it *The Book of Life.*

Collier's "Secret of the Ages" was this: From earliest time, humanity has possessed the ability to invent, build, and advance through the creative energies of thought. Man's mental power, Collier explained, is a metaphysical *force* that lifted humankind out of caves and into the light of fire; it created the ancient civilizations of Egypt, Mesopotamia, and the Indus Valley; it built the empires of Greece and Rome; and its powers are encrypted in the ancient narratives, parabolic or otherwise, of every miracle from Aladdin's Lamp to Christ's walking on water.

Collier could be startlingly blunt about his views. "Mind is God," he wrote in 1927. "And the subconscious in us is our part of Divinity." But he was never cavalier. Collier expressed deep reverence for the teachings of Christ, which he considered a psychological blueprint to man's highest potential.

The metaphysical insights that aided Collier's recovery did not render him impervious to disease. He died of intestinal cancer in 1950, two years after revising and expanding *The Secret of the Ages*. But the facts of his and our physical limits should not engender cynicism toward Collier's work. His writing sparkles with sincerity and discovery, which is preserved in this condensation of his key principles. His ideas have contributed to the success of a wide range of readers, many of whom wrote to Collier during his lifetime, and have continued to make *The Secret of the Ages* a cornerstone of self-development literature in the decades since his passing.

—Mitch Horowitz

Chapter One

The World's Greatest Discovery

What, in your opinion, is the most significant discovery of our age? The finding of dinosaur eggs on the plains of Mongolia laid some 100,000,000 years ago? The unearthing of ancient tombs and cities with their specimens of bygone civilizations? The radioactive time clock by which we can estimate the age of earth at 4.5 billion years?

No—none of these. The really significant thing about this vast research from the study of bygone ages is that for the first time we are beginning to understand the existence of a "Vital Force" that—somehow, some way—was brought to earth millions of years ago.

It matters not whether you believe that mankind dates back to the primitive ape-man or sprang full-grown from the mind of the Creator. In either event, there had to be a First Cause—a source of Creation. Some Power had to bring to earth the first germ of Life.

No one can follow history down through the ages without realizing that the whole purpose of existence is GROWTH. Life is dynamic. It is ever moving forward. The one unpardonable sin of nature is to stand still, to stagnate.

Egypt and Persia, Greece and Rome, all the great empires of antiquity perished *when they ceased to grow.*

It is for men and women who refuse to stand still that this book is written. It will give you a clear understanding of your own potential, and show you how to work with and take advantage of the creative energy that surrounds you.

The evidence of this energy is everywhere. Take up some rigorous exercise—rowing, tennis, swimming, riding. In the beginning your muscles are weak, easily tired. But keep at it for a few days. The Vital Force flows into them more strongly, strengthens them, toughens them. Do rough manual labor—and what happens? The skin of your hands becomes tender, blisters, hurts. Keep it up and the Vital Force provides extra thickness, extra toughness—calluses, we call them—to meet your need.

All through daily life you will find this Life Force steadily at work. Embrace it, work with it, take it to yourself, and there is nothing you cannot do.

The fact that you have obstacles to overcome is in your favor. For when there is nothing to be done, when things run along too smoothly, this Life Force seems to sleep. It is when you need it, when you call upon it urgently, when you seem to have used up every reserve in you, that it is most on the job.

The Life Force makes no distinction between rich and poor, high and low. The greater your need, the more readily will it respond to your call. Wherever there is an unusual task, wherever there is poverty, hardship, sickness, or despair, *there* is this Servant of your Mind, ready and eager to help, asking only that you call upon it.

Chapter Two

Your Higher Self

The power to be what you want, to get what you desire, to accomplish whatever you are striving for, abides within you. It rests with you only to bring it forth. You must learn how to do that, of course, but the first essential is to *realize that you possess this power.*

You are not a mere clod. You are not a beast of burden relegated to spend your days in unremitting labor in return for food and housing. You are one of the Lords of the Earth, with unlimited potentialities. Within you is a power that, properly grasped and directed, can lead you out of mediocrity and place you among the elect—the lawgivers, the writers, the engineers, the great industrialists—the DOERS and the THINKERS. It rests with you to learn to use this Universal Mind that can do all things.

Carl Jung claimed that the subconscious contains not only all the knowledge that it has gathered during the life of the individual, but that it also contains all the wisdom of past ages. And that by drawing on its wisdom and power the individual may possess any good and noble thing of life.

You see, the subconscious is the connecting link between the Creator and ourselves, between Vital Force and our own bodies and affairs.

Most of us think of mind as merely the conscious part of us. But the earliest Greek religious writings taught that man is a triune being: *first*, the physical or conscious self; *second*, the subconscious, sometimes called your "Inner Mind" because it is latent within you; and *third*, the superconscious or "Higher Self."

Go back 2,000 years before Christ to the Upanishads, the earliest religious books of India, and you find a similar teaching. Study the religion of the Egyptians and you find the same belief. The great pyramids were triangular on each side, exemplifying the idea you find on many of their monuments. The Egyptians believed that the "Ka," or "Higher Self" could separate itself from the body and perform any service required of it.

You can send your Higher Self to do your will. Through it, you can protect your loved ones, you can heal, you can help in all ways.

To do so, however, you must charge the situation with your own Vital Force. You can never help another without giving something of yourself. You must consciously GIVE of your Vital Force. You must have the faith to SEE your Higher Self doing the things that you direct it to do. You must BELIEVE that it IS doing them. Given such faith, all things are possible to you.

YOU are a Creator, with the God-given power to use that Vital Force as you please. But to create *anything of good* requires four things:

1. The mental image of what you want. That is the mold.

2. Knowledge of your power, so you can consciously draw to you all the Vital Force you need—breathe it in—and then pour it into your mental mold.

3. Faith in your creative power, faith to crystalize the Vital Force into your mold, until it is manifest for all to see.

4. Doing something to convince your subconscious mind—and, through it, the superconscious—that you *believe you HAVE received*. For instance, a woman who prayed for a house got a board and nail and kept them before her, affirming that they were the beginning of the house.

As I see it, the Universal Mind is the Supreme Intelligence and Creator of the Universe, and we are partakers of the Divine Attributes. You are part of it, I am part of it, and anything we do *that is for the good of all* has the support of this Universal Mind—*provided we call upon it.*

CHAPTER THREE

The Primal Cause

G ive me a base of support," said Archimedes, "and with a lever I will move the world."

Your base of support is *mind*. All started with mind. In the beginning was nothing—a fire mist. Before anything could come out of it there had to be an *idea,* a model upon which to build. *Universal Mind* supplied that idea. Therefore the primal cause is mind. Everything must start with an idea.

Matter in the ultimate is but a product of thought. Even the most materialist scientists acknowledge that matter is not as it appears. According to physics, matter, be it the human body or a log of wood, is an aggregation of distinct minute particles or atoms.

Until fairly recently, these atoms were supposed to be the ultimate makeup of matter. We ourselves—and all the material world—were supposed to consist of these infinitesimal particles, so small that they could not be seen, weighed, or touched individually—but, still, particles of matter *and indestructible.*

Now, however, these atoms have been further analyzed; and physics tells us that they are not indestructible at all—that they are mere positive and negative buttons of force or energy called protons and electrons, without hardness, without density, without solidity, without even positive actuality. In short, they are vortices in the ether—whirling bits of energy—dynamic, never static, pulsating with life.

And that, mind you, is what the solid table in front of you is made of, is what your house, your body, and the whole world is made of—*whirling bits of energy!*

Your body is about 85 percent water, 15 percent ash, phosphorus, and other elements. And they, in turn, can be dissipated into gas and vapor. Where do we go from there?

Is not the answer that, to a great degree at least, and perhaps altogether, this world is *one of our mind's own creating*?

Reduced to the ultimate—to the atom or to the electron—everything in this world is an idea of mind. All of it has been brought together through mind.

The world without is but a reflection of the world within. Your thought *creates* the conditions that the mind images. Keep before your mind's eye the image of all you want to be, and you will see it reflected in the world without.

Few of us have any idea of our mental powers. The *old idea* was that man must take this world as he found it. The basis of all democracies is that man is *not* bound by any system, that he need not accept the world as he finds it. He can remake the world to his own ideas.

As French psychologist Charles Baudouin puts it, "You will go in the direction in which you face..."

This new principle is responsible for all our inventions, all our progress. Man is satisfied with nothing. He is constantly remaking his world.

But there *must be an idea* before it can take form. As psychologist Terry Walter says: "The impressions that enter the subconscious form indelible pictures, which are never forgotten, and whose power can change the body, mind, manner, and morals; can, in fact, revolutionize a personality."

Learn to control your thoughts. Learn to image upon your mind only the things you want to see reflected there. Your thoughts supply you with limitless energy that will take whatever form your mind demands.

Begin at once, today, to use what you have learned. All growth comes from practice. All the forces of life are active—peace—joy—power.

You are "heir of God and coheir with Christ." And as such, no evil has power over you, whereas you have all power for good. And "good" means not merely holiness. Good means happiness—the happiness of everyday people.

CHAPTER FOUR

This One Thing I Do

It may sound paradoxical, but few people really know what they want.

Most of them struggle along in a vague sort of way, hoping for something to turn up. They are so occupied with the struggle that they have forgotten—if they ever knew—what they are struggling *for*. They are like a drowning man, using up many times the energy it would take to get somewhere, frittering it away in aimless struggles—without thought or direction.

You must know what you want before you stand any chance of getting it.

How did the Salvation Army get so much favorable publicity out of the First World War? They were a comparatively small part of the "services" that catered to the boys, yet they carried off the lion's share of the glory. Do you know how they did it?

By concentrating on just one thing—DOUGH-NUTS!

They served doughnuts to the boys—and they did it *well*. And that is the basis of all success in business and in most parts of life: to focus on one thing and do that thing well. Better by far to do one thing preeminently well than to dabble in forty.

The greatest success rule I know in business—the one that should be printed over everyone's desk is—"This One Thing I Do."

Volumes have been written about personal efficiency. But boiled down, it all comes to six steps:

1. Know what you want.
2. Analyze the thing you must do to get it.
3. Plan your work ahead.
4. Do one thing at a time.
5. Finish that one thing and send it on its way before starting the next.
6. Once started, KEEP GOING!

In the realm of mind, the realm of all practical power, you can possess what you want at once. You have but to claim it, visualize it, and believe in it to bring it into actuality. And all you need to begin this process is an earnest, intense, well-focused DESIRE.

"But," you will say, "I have plenty of desires. I've always wanted to be rich. How do you account for difference between my wealth, position, and power and that of the rich men all around me?"

The problem is simply that you have never focused your desires into *one great dominating desire.* You have a host of mild desires. You mildly wish you were rich, you wish you had a position of responsibility and influence, you wish you could travel at will. The wishes are so many and so varied that they conflict with each other and you get nowhere in particular. You lack one *intense* desire, to which you are willing to subordinate everything else.

Take one idea, make a good distinct picture of it, and immediately your thoughts begin to group themselves, and you have the nucleus of your desire. *This one thing you do*, and ideas from the SELF within begin to collect around the one thing, and you open the way for your good to flow to you.

Watch your thoughts! Examine each thought that comes to you. It may be your calling. Open your mind, be alert to the things happening around you. Be interested in everyone you meet; you may entertain an angel unawares. He may have a vital message for you, or you for him. Watch for your special work, recognize it, be ready for it. And when it arrives equip yourself to excel in it through study, application, and arduous practice. And, above all, *focus your efforts on this one thing.*

Do you know how Napoleon so frequently won battles in the face of a numerically superior foe? By concentrating his men at the actual *point of contact!* His artillery was often greatly outnumbered, but it accomplished far more than the enemy's because instead of scattering his fire, he *concentrated it all on the point of attack!*

The time you spend aimlessly dreaming and wishing would accomplish marvels if it were concentrated upon one definite object.

If you want a thing badly enough you will have no trouble concentrating on it. Your thoughts will naturally center on it, like bees on honey.

In his ESP experiments at Duke University, Dr. J.B. Rhine demonstrated that the mind can definitely influence inanimate objects, but only when there is intense interest or desire. When the subject's interest was distracted, when he failed to concentrate his attention, he had no power over the object. It was only as he gave his entire attention to it, concentrated his every energy upon it, that he got successful results.

Dr. Rhine proved through physical experiments what most of us have always believed: that there *is* a Power over and above the merely physical powers of the mind or body; that through intense concentration we can line up with that Power; and that once we do, nothing is impossible to us.

CHAPTER FIVE

Universal Mind

It is not always the man who struggles hardest who wins. It is the direction as well as the energy of the struggle that counts.

To get ahead you must swim with the tide. Those who prosper and succeed work in accord with natural forces. A given amount of effort with these forces carries a man faster and farther than much more effort used *against the current*. Those who work blindly, regardless of these forces, make life difficult for themselves and rarely prosper.

It has been estimated that something like 60 percent of the factors producing success or failure lie outside of a man's conscious efforts—separate from his daily round of details. To the extent that he cooperates with the wisdom and power of Universal Mind he is successful, well, and happy. To the extent that he fails to cooperate, he is unsuccessful, sick, and miserable.

The connecting link between your conscious mind and Universal Mind is *thought*. And every thought that is in harmony with progress and good, every thought that is freighted with the right idea, can penetrate to Universal Mind. And penetrating to the Universal Mind, your thought returns with the power of Universal Mind to accomplish it. You don't need to originate the ways and means. The Universal Mind knows how to bring about any necessary results.

There is one right way to solve any problem. When your human judgment is unable to decide what that one right way is, turn to Universal Mind for guidance. You need never fear the outcome; if you heed its advice you cannot go astray.

A flash of genius does not originate in your own brain. Through intense concentration you establish a circuit through your subconscious mind with the Universal, and it is from the Higher Mind that the inspiration comes. All genius, all progress comes from this same source.

CHAPTER SIX

See Yourself Doing It

What does it mean that *God created man in His own image*?

"The imagination," writes Glenn Clark in *The Soul's Sincere Desire*, "is of all the qualities in man the most Godlike—that which associates him most closely with God. The first mention we read of man in the Bible is where he is spoken of as an 'image.' 'Let us make man in our own image, after our likeness.' The only place where an image can be conceived is in the imagination."

If man was made in God's image, it stands to reason that man's imagination—like that of the Great Master—is capable of creation.

When you form a mental image of the good you wish to come to pass, make it clear, picture it vividly in every detail, BELIEVE in it, and the "Genie-of-Your-Mind" will bring it into being as an everyday reality.

The keynote of successful visualization is this: *See things as you would have them be instead of as they are.*

Close your eyes and make clear mental pictures. Make them look and act just as they would in real life. In short, daydream—but daydream with a *purpose*. Better still, get those pictures down on paper using, if you need to, pictures of similar things cut from magazines. Concentrate on one idea at a time to the exclusion of others, and continue to concentrate on that one idea until it has been accomplished.

Chapter Seven

The Formula of Success

What is the eternal question that stands up and looks you and every sincere person squarely in the eye each morning?

"How can I better my condition?" That is the real-life question that confronts you, and will haunt you every day till you solve it.

Often this question takes the form of whether you should stick to the job you have, or seek a better one. The answer depends entirely on what you are striving for. The first thing is to set your goal. What is it you want? A profession? A political career? An executive position? A business of your own?

Every position should yield you three things:

1. Reasonable pay for the present.
2. Knowledge, training, or experience that will be worth money to you in the future.

3. Prestige or acquaintances that will be of assistance in attaining your goal.

Judge every opening by these three standards. But don't overlook chances for valuable training, merely because the pay is small.

Some complain of their station in life and feel that their surroundings are discouraging. Do you feel that if you were in another's place success would be easier? Just bear in mind that your real environment is *within you*. All the factors of success or failure are in your inner world. *You* make your own inner world—and through it your outer world. You can choose the material from which to build. If you have chosen unwisely in the past, you can choose new material now. The richness of life is within you. Start right in and do all those things you feel you have it in you to do. *Ask permission of no one.*

Take the first step and your mind will mobilize all of its forces to your aid. But it is essential is that you *begin.*

Those who have made their mark on life all had one trait in common: they *believed in themselves.* "But," you may ask, "how can I believe in myself when I have never done anything worthwhile, when everything I put my hand to seems to fail?" You can't, of course. That is, you couldn't if you had to depend upon your conscious mind alone. But remember what one far greater than you said: "I can of mine own self do nothing. The Father that is within me—He doeth the works."

That same "Father" is within you. And it is by knowing that He *is* in you, and that through Him you can do anything that is right, that you can acquire the belief in yourself that is so necessary.

The starting point is *Faith*. But St. James tells us: "Faith without works is dead." So go on to the next step. Decide the one thing you want most from life. No matter what it may be. There is no limit to Mind. Visualize this thing that you want. See it, feel it, BELIEVE in it. Make your mental blueprint, and *begin to build!*

Psychologists have discovered that the best time to make suggestions to your subconscious is just before going to sleep, when the senses are quiet and the body is relaxed. So, let us take your desire and suggest it to your subconscious mind tonight. The two prerequisites are the earnest DESIRE, and an intelligent, understanding BELIEF.

Do that every night until you ACTUALLY DO BELIEVE that you have the thing you want. When you reach that point, *YOU WILL HAVE IT!*

Chapter Eight

The Law of Attraction

Look around you. What businesses are getting ahead? Who are the big successes? Are they the ones who grab the passing dollar, careless of what they offer in return? Or are they those who are striving always to give a little greater value, a little more work than they are paid for?

When scales are balanced evenly, a trifle of extra weight thrown on either side overbalances the other as effectively as a ton.

In the same way, a little better value, a little extra effort, makes the man of business stand out from the great mass of mediocrity, and brings results out of all proportion to the additional effort involved.

It pays—not merely altruistically, but in good, hard dollars—to give a little more value than seems necessary, to work a bit harder than you are paid for. It's that extra ounce of value that counts.

For, the Law of Attraction is service. We receive in proportion as we give out. In fact, we usually receive in far greater proportion.

"Whosoever shall be great among you," said Jesus, "shall be your minister, and whosoever of you will be the chiefest, shall be the servant of all." In other words, if you would be great, you must serve. And he who serves most shall be greatest of all.

If you want to make more money, instead of seeking it for yourself see how you can make more for others. In the process you will inevitably make more for yourself, too. We get as we give. *But we must give first.*

It matters not where you start—you may be a day laborer. But still you can give—give a bit more of energy, of work, of thought, than you are paid for. Try to put a little extra skill into your work. Use your mind to find some better way of doing whatever task may be set for you.

There is no kind of work or method that cannot be improved by thought. So give generously of your thought to your work. Think every minute you are at it: "Isn't there some way this could be done easier, quicker, better?" Read everything that relates to your own work, or to the job ahead of you.

Look around YOU now. How can YOU give greater value for what you get? How can you SERVE better?

How can you make more money for your employers, or save more for your customers? Keep that thought ever in front of you and *you'll never need to worry about making more money for yourself.*

CHAPTER NINE

Your Needs Are Met

n old man called his children to his bedside to give them a few parting words of advice. "My children," he said, "I have had a great deal of trouble in my life—a great deal of trouble—*but most of it never happened.*"

We are all like that old man. Our troubles weigh us down, in prospect, but we usually find that when the actual need arrives, Providence has devised some way of meeting it.

In moments of great peril, in times of extremity, when the brave soul has staked its all—those are the times when miracles are wrought, if we but have faith.

That does not mean that you should rest supinely at your ease and let the Lord provide. When you have done *all that is in you to do*—when you have given your very best—don't worry or fret as to the outcome. Know that if more is needed, your need will be met. You can sit back with the confident assurance that, having done your part, you can depend upon the Genie-of-Your-Mind to do the rest.

This does not mean that you will never have difficulties. Difficulties are good for you. They are the exercise of your mind. You are the stronger for having overcome them. But look upon them as mere exercise, as "stunts" that are given you in order to better learn how to use your mind, and how to draw upon Universal Supply. Like Jacob wrestling with the Angel, don't let your difficulties go until they have blessed you—until, in other words, you have learned something from having encountered them.

Chapter Ten

The Master Mind

The Transcendentalist philosopher Ralph Waldo Emerson wrote: "There is one mind common to all individual men. Every man is an inlet to the same and to all of the same. He that is once admitted to the right of reason is made a freeman of the whole estate. What Plato has thought, he may think; what a saint has felt, he may feel; what at any time has befallen any man, he can understand. Who hath access to this universal mind is a party to all that is or can be done, for this is the only and sovereign agent."

The great German physicist Walther Nernst found that the longer an electric current was made to flow through a filament, the greater became the conductivity of the filament.

In the same way, the more you call upon and use your subconscious mind, the greater becomes its conductivity in passing along to you the infinite resources of Universal Mind. The wisdom of a Solomon, the skill of Michelangelo, the genius of an Edison, the daring of a Napoleon, *all* may be yours. It rests with you only to form contact with Universal Mind in order to draw from it what you will.

Think of this power as something that you can connect with at any time. It has the answer to all of your problems. There is no reason why you should hesitate to aspire to any position, any honor, any goal, for the Mind within you is fully able to meet any need. It is no more difficult for it to handle a great problem than a small one. Mind is just as much present in your everyday affairs as in those of a big business or a great nation.

Start something! Use your initiative. Give your mind something to work upon. The greatest of all success secrets is *initiative*. It is the one quality, more than any other, that has put men in high places.

Conceive something. Conceive it first in your own mind. Make the pattern there and your superconscious mind will draw upon the plastic substance or energy all about you to make that model real.

The connecting link between the human and the Divine, between the formed universe and formless energy, lies in your imaging faculty. It is, of all things human, the most God-like. It is our part of Divinity. Through it we share in the creative power of Universal

Mind. Through it we can turn the drabbest existence into a thing of life and beauty. It is the means by which we avail ourselves of all the good that the Universal Mind is constantly offering.

When Jesus adjured His disciples, "whatsoever ye desire, when ye pray, believe that ye RECEIVE it," He was not only telling them a great truth, but he was teaching what we moderns would call excellent psychology, as well. For this "belief" is what acts upon the subconscious mind and through it upon the superconscious. It is through this "belief" that formless energy is compressed into material form.

The Apostles were almost all poor, uneducated men, yet they did a work that is unequalled in history. Joan of Arc was a poor, illiterate peasant girl—yet she saved France. So don't allow lack of training, lack of education, to hold you back. Your mind can meet every need, and direct you to every necessary step.

The pages of history are filled with ordinary people who went on to think great thoughts, forge great nations, build and invent great things, and became religious, political, or commercial leaders. *Begin now.* Use the glorious empire of your mind to build that which you yearn to see in the world, that which would help yourself and others.

Use the infinite horizons of your mind—a part of the Universal Mind, a part of Divinity.

About the Authors

Born in St. Louis, Missouri, in 1885, ROBERT COLLIER trained for the priesthood before entering a career in business. He achieved success in the fields of advertising, publishing, and engineering. After struggling with a severe and chronic case of food poisoning, Collier recovered using methods of Christian Science, New Thought, prayer therapy, and autosuggestion. He made an intensive study of the new metaphysics and distilled what he learned into a popular and influential pamphlet series first called *The Book of Life* in 1925 and renamed *The Secret of the Ages* in 1926. Collier assembled *The Secret of the Ages* into a single volume, which he revised and expanded in 1948. The author of many books on the mystical dimensions of the mind, Collier died in 1950.

MITCH HOROWITZ, who abridged and introduced this volume, is the PEN Award-winning author of books including *Occult America* and *The Miracle Club: How Thoughts Become Reality*. *The Washington Post* says Mitch "treats esoteric ideas and movements with an even-handed intellectual studiousness that is too often lost in today's raised-voice discussions." Follow him @MitchHorowitz.